I0159856

Drops of Rain and Grains of Sand

Drops of Rain and Grains of Sand

A collection of thoughts

Michael Fleming/Brahmacharya Baba

Distributed in the USA, Canada and Mexico
by Amazon.com

Published by Michaels Rainbow

Copyright © 2017
by Michael Fleming/Brahmacharya Baba
All rights reserved.

ISBN: 978-0-9910130-2-9

Printed in the United States of America

ACKNOWLEDGMENTS

Edited by:
Steve Hoffmann who always pulls out the greatest in me

And Sidney Chriqui,
a friend who also understands what I am saying.

Joseph (Buddy) Bean for
Me, My Brother and I cover drawing

Cover and art by Michael Fleming

A few comments from friends
who have previewed my book

Drops of Rain and Grains of Sand is not a book you can pick up and read cover to cover. It is a collection of intensely personal introspective revelations by the author, made over many years of life's experiences that run the gamut of human existence. Some observations are universal truths that will be understood and appreciated by all. Some possess deeper and more complex meanings that must be pondered and savored before realization is achieved and appreciated. Some others are so purely personal to the author that they require the reader to project themselves into the mind of the author to gain understanding ... and that, of course, is his purpose.
Put this on your nightstand and read a page a day ... it's worth the inspiration.

Jon Michael - Bradfordsville, Kentucky

You wrote a very beautiful work and I would like to thank you for allowing me to read it first. I find it to be very interesting and quite challenging for any reader.
The reader will enjoy the poetic beauty of the many guides that Mr. Fleming cites - you feel very much his generous approach, to share his true feelings with us.

Sidney Chriqui, North Hollywood, California

I have read the draft with keen interest. It is not only interesting but it gives a feeling of genuine works coming straight from the heart.

Bibhash Bhaduri, Varanasi, India

The book is only a small one but it is deep, meaningful and philosophical. I don't have any particular comment to offer but without least hesitation I should say that I loved it. It is not for easy reading and needs deep insight to understand its philosophy. You have to deal with subjects like, tears, love, happiness and sadness as well.

Soumitra Basu, New Delhi, India,

Michael Fleming's Drops of Rain and Grains of Sand is a poetic collection of wisdom, creativity and beauty. One may find themselves dwelling less on life's disappointments, and instead opening their mind to life's treasures. Truly a wonderful experience.

Jacqueline Mobley, North Hollywood, Ca

Your poetry is a delight ...
I see the sweetness of your own mouth, and want what you already have...
I ponder on these things while reading your Drops of Rain and Grains of Sand.
The more I know, the more there is [to know]...
Know yourself within others.
I know when I am a bastard and not sure I want to hear it from anyone ...
You are in constant evolution/revolution. Standing still ... never!
(To) Give unsolicited advice is rarely welcomed.
Man and flower are equal, they have different purpose in creation.

Claire Sarradet, Grande-Valle, Québec Canada

Authors introduction

My first book, *Follow Your Heart* tells a story of me as I transformed from one of the first computer programmers in the world ... into a hippie.

It was the 1960s and LSD (acid) was being used all around me. I tried it once, then again and yet again.

While others were taking the trip on acid; seeing paisley patterns, having fun and dancing around, I went into my mind and met, faced, then revealed to my friends, dark and difficult events that had been hiding behind blinders in my mind.

By honestly revealing the ugliness that I was seeing I was also slowly conquering the demons of my past.

After taking these trips for a year or so, there was nothing left to face or accept, conquer or hide.I saw the inside of my brain as a shiny and clean container without cobwebs or darkness of the past.

Then a vision came upon me, it was so vast and overwhelming that my body was physically shaking. I called that vision ... God. No, it wasn't a man with a flowing beard that people sometimes picture; the word *picture* is what confuses. Perhaps *experienced* is the better word, but it still cannot be disclosed in a few short sentences.

Several months after the vision I changed into another person, and began to live a totally different life. I quit my job gave my house and all of my belongings away; left most of my friends behind and "stepped out," as the Hippies used to say, and became a Hippie. As I left my house behind, I stepped into a different world as a different person.

As time passed, other lives and other worlds unfolded. I also changed with each life of course.

To some left behind it was as if I had died. Perhaps it is as I have written; that I have lived many lives in this living, without the laying down of my body.

Follow Your Heart is a story of these times .

My journey wasn't only about the physical events that unfolded however; my mind and my thinking were changing as well.

I lived, learned and grew from the programmer into a multi-dimensional being.

I began to write soon after the vision and continued to write as I moved through different lives and my understandings grew.

My writing style was inspired by the book, *Sand and Foam* by Kahlil Gibran; who taught me that the placement of words had as much impact as the punctuation.

Here, catch.- -

- - Got it.

During the time between the vision of god/God (as I prefer to call it) and leaving the house behind, I wrote a small book of inspired aphorisms which I called, *Me, My Brother and I*. I made about 30 copies of it to share with friends.

As it happens I left for Europe a few months later and spent four months there with a Eurail pass and back pack, Europe at that time, was awash with Hippies, Love Children, Flower Children or what ever the current turn would name us.

I took the copies of my book with me, as well as beads to make "love beads" as gifts to people I would meet while journeying into my new life.

Drops of Rain and Grains of Sand begins with this small book, *Me, My Brother and I* as Part 1.
I wrote Part 2 while touring Europe, and called it, *On the Tail of the Dragon*.

Returning from Europe I began another life. The final chapter - - *And life goes on*, are writings that continue from there.

As Follow Your Heart is an account of my physical journeys, Drops of Rain and Grains of Sand is a collection of spiritual writings I wrote as I physically lived those lives.

Growing as we all grow, my writings reflect these changes. Welcome to the unfolding world of this wonderful journey.

Drops of Rain and Grains of Sand

Part 1 - Me, My Brother and I

Written after having a vision which I called God
and finished just before I left for Europe
as a Hippie.

Part 2 - On the tail of the Dragon

Written as I traveled around Europe
with a back pack and a Eurail pass
for 4 months.

Part 3 - And life goes on

And life does indeed go on.
This last part was written after I returned
to the United States to begin living the lives
that unfolded from then until now.

✤

Part 1

Me, My Brother and I

Dedicated to the thought which is the beginning and the end.

"I am my brother, not his brother".

Claude J, Mower

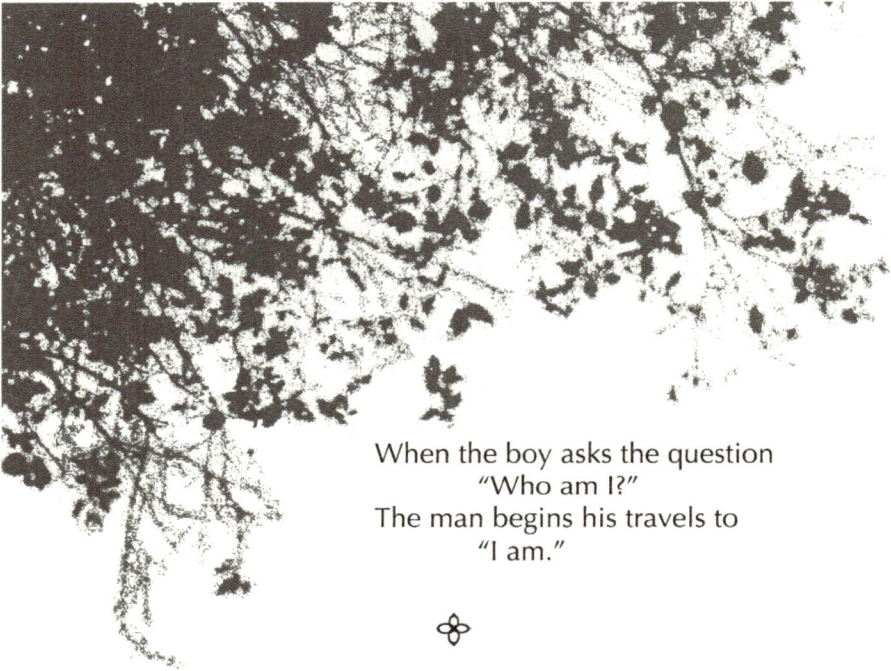

When the boy asks the question
            "Who am I?"
The man begins his travels to
            "I am."

❖

    Where am I going?
Forward slowly, sometimes backwards\
        hopefully never standing still.

Knowing (not knowledge) is my goal.
        Where is it?
I don't know yet,
        but when I do know
            I will already be there.

Love:
    That you might be loved.
Give:
    That you might receive.
Empathize:
    That you might be understood.
Cry:
    That you might know joy.
Teach:
    That you might learn.
Heal:
    That you might be made whole.
Listen::
    That you might know yourself within others.
And allow others to do likewise:
    That you might partake of these blessings.

✤

Eat sometimes of a lemon
    that you might know the sweetness
    of your own mouth.

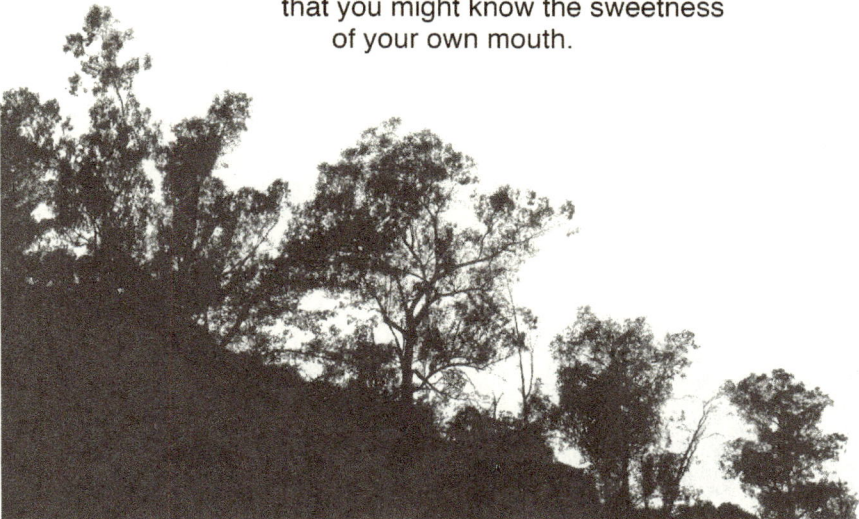

A poor man held out his hand for help.
Though my hand was empty also
I offered it in aid.
We clasped hands and lo;
    both hands were filled.

❀

It is good to speak to the mountain,
    for you cannot say, "You lie,"
    to an echo.

❀

With fanfare and beating of drums that shakes the world,
    Love - -
        gently whispers of its being.

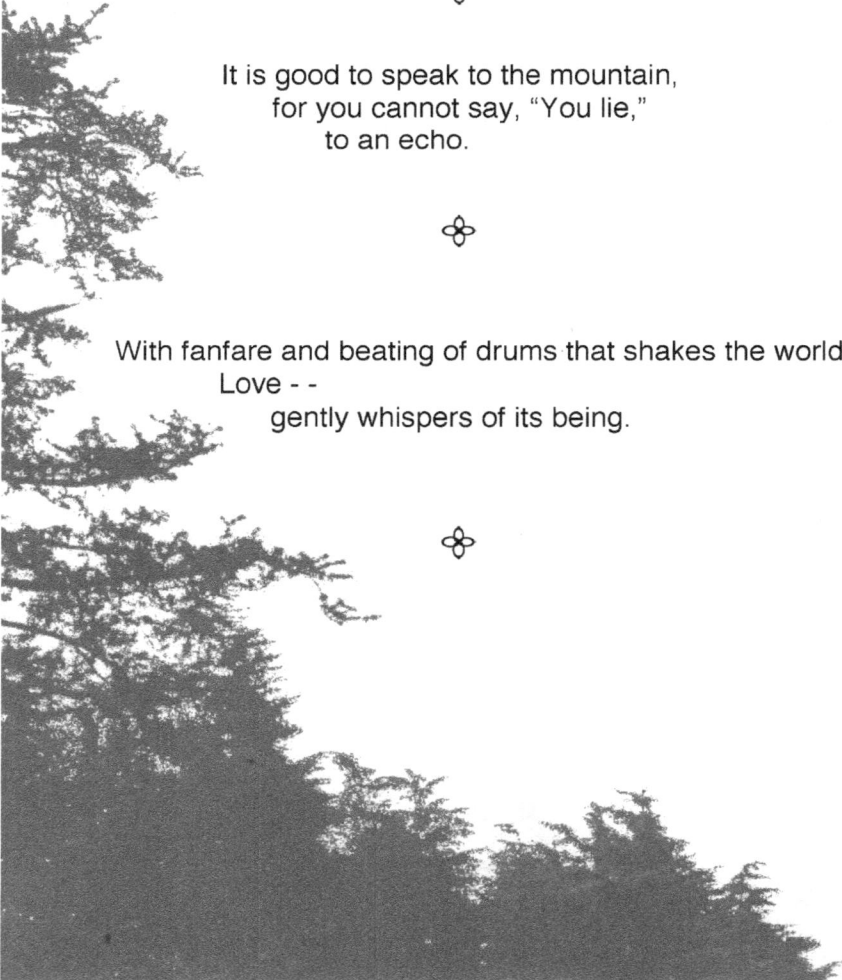

❀

If you aren't happy with what you are doing
would it not be wise to do that which makes you happy?
Ah - but that would be too simple.

❖

I have offended;
I do it all the time,
but my friends love me so much they won't tell.
Thus I still offend.
I wish - -
someone loved me enough to call me a bastard,

❖

Talent
is love, patience and desire
activated,
nothing more.

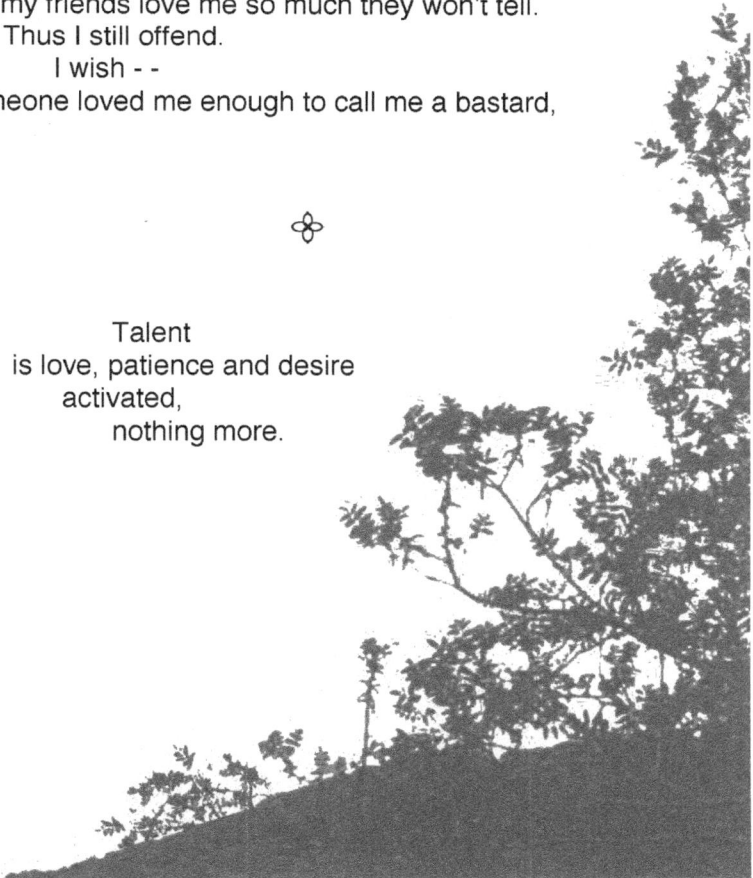

Your advice is kindly taken - -
but how can you give it so freely
when you don't even know
where I'm going?

❖

The play is not played for one person alone,
situations exist for us all.
The good and the bad like magnets they draw
each of us as we need
for the rise or the fall.

❖

Even giving a crust of bread from a poor man
is giving a part of himself that could have been.
How much deeper then, must the rich man dig into his treasures
to give such a gift?

❖

A gift twice given
is love twice shared.

Please don't ask me to bend to your ways.
Show me instead
the truth of where you stand;
then I will move,
and still stand straight.

⚜

Man travels the road from "Who am I?" to "I am,"
The children play somewhere behind
- - and ahead.

⚜

Isn't man a wonderful thing?
Who else can hold his head so high
that even he cannot see over it?

⚜

Life is all of your yesterdays
- - fulfilled;
and the groundwork
for all your tomorrows.

If you love me, - -
please repeat back what I have said;
for perhaps - -
I wasn't listening.

❖

You cannot understand or believe that we are One:
And yet, I cannot understand how you could believe
that you are not part of the whole.

❖

Many times
being born again is little more than
letting go of the past.

Love begets love;
　　it feeds upon itself
　　　　and grows from its excesses.
But first it must be given
　　before it "is".

❖

Each of us has their own message to give to the world;
　　each is different, each is complete.
　　　　Yet, - -
combine two of them, or four, or even more
　　and a new message is created;
　　　　still different, still complete,
　　　　　　and ready to be joined with others,
　　　　　　　　for thus is the eternal plan.

❖

　　　　Life, - - it seems,
　　　is that portion of our existence
　　　　dedicated most to avoiding
　　　　　　that which is called living.

A mountain is a molehill
for which someone cared.

✧

In every hell is a bit of heaven,
and and therin lies our salvation.
In every heaven is a bit of hell,
and therein lies our growth.

✧

It is good that my eyes can speak - -
for without them,
you might think my mouth
speaks falsely.

✧

You are a mirror to me of my own image.
    Stay then awhile if I have not seen your beauty;
that I might find in you, that part of myself
    which I find ugly
        and keeps me from seeing your beauty.

⚜

First you must pour of your wine,
    only then will your cup be filled.

⚜

Yesterday is no more. - -
    Tomorrow is not, as yet.
        There is only now.
Now is forever and forever is now.
    Forever is ever limited by that which we do now.
Is it not now then, to do that which is to be?

I know that I am only a part of the things that surround me.
        And yet, - - somehow I know
            that these same things are also parts of
                and even wholes of
                    - - myself.

⊹

            Please - -
        don't make me stand in your shadow,
    for don't you see how much larger it is than you?

⊹

                There was a time I think,
                    when we thought not
                        and love was real.
                But love I think was thought away.
                    I think I should't thin,
                        - - but feel.

It is not the question,
    nor is it the answer,
        but the means to get from one to the other
           that causes living.

                        ❖

Turn not your eyes from a stranger,
    for from his eyes shine forth
        yet another part
           of that which you are.

                        ❖

Be that which is your enemy
    for one day, or one hour;
        then would you not make war
           - - upon yourself?

                        ❖

If only we could love ourselves
how much lighter would be our paths.

It is not that I love you or I love me,
    it is only that I love.

✧

Is it not a thing of beauty
that the selfish are never content with what they have?
    And is it not also just and fair
that they must learn to give those things which they have
        before they will ever know the joy of true having?

✧

Look at me - -
        please;
    not at my mouth which spews forth lies
        to protect me, - - from myself.

✧

Love - -
Is the sweetest kiss of springtime,
    with poison on its lips
        that we might die
        and be born again - -
        to love.

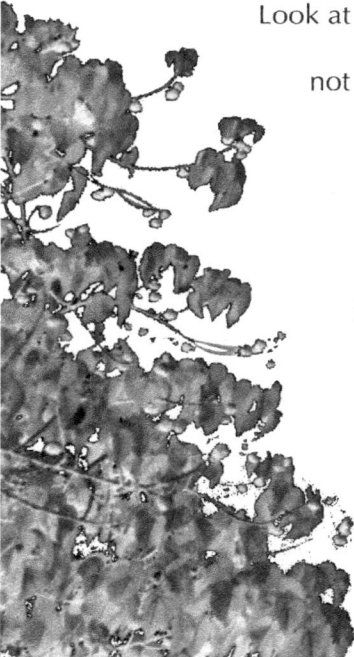

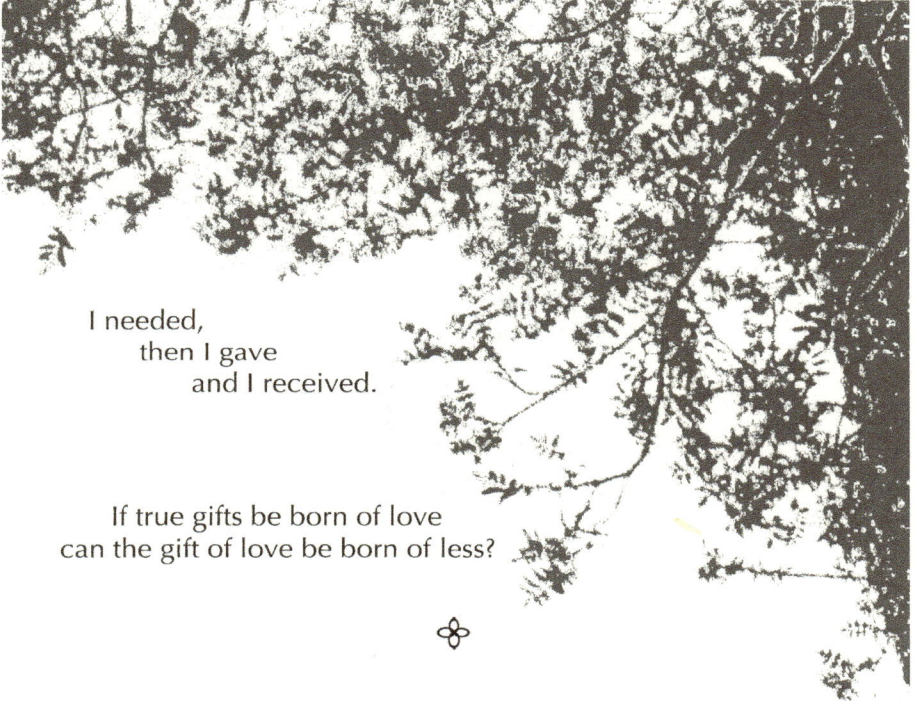

I needed,
then I gave
and I received.

If true gifts be born of love
can the gift of love be born of less?

❧

It doesn't matter what you say
as long as you feel what you say
and say what you feel;
truth will be found.

❧

Be that which you are,
for can you not be better those things that are yourself
than that which is no part of you?

Let yourself be all things
that you might love all things
- - and in turn be loved.

⟡

I have no more pride
I have no more shame;
for that which I am, - -
we all are the same.

⟡

I was there but you did not see.
I called but you did not hear.
I loved, and you knew.

⟡

Death - -
is like riding into the sunset
- - of the sunrise.

A poet once exclaimed to a scholar;
"Quick, look into the mirror and see your God."
The scholar looked, but saw only himself.
Then the poet looked again,
and saw all things.

❧

I would like to make you smile - -
that you might see me smiling.

❧

Most communication is not me to you
or you to me;
rather it is me to me and you to you
in front of each other - -
that we might show our beilif
in the words that we are saying
- - to ourselves.

The price of possessions is freedom,
and it continues to be
as long as we possess.

❖

We fear -
    that we might overcome.
Overcome -
    that we might understand.
Understand -
    that we might know.
Know -
    that we might love.
And love -
    that we might be.

❖

There is more riddle to life
    and life to riddle
        than all the philosophers and fools can see.

❖

There once was a flower that bloomed within a field of weeds.
It gave beauty and love to those who might become discouraged
      at seeing so many weeds.
One day a man came upon the flower
      and felt that the flower did not belong there among the weeds,
            so he picked the one thing of beauty within the field.
The flower would now die, but if the man would absorb its beauty
      and remember its love, it could have life again
            through the very one who had cut its life short.
The flower felt its life ebbing and whispered to the man,
      "Quick, while there is still time, let me become more of you."
The flower then quietly died, never knowing if it would live on.
      And as I watched the man walk away
            I wondered upon the same thought.

And the weeds thought, "Hey, where'd our flower go?"

                              ⌗

                  Thoughts
      are the only living drops of blood within us
            to which we can give eternal life.

                              ⌗

God is all things
and all things are true.
Even lies can be lived out to their truth.

⚜

Please - -
let me look at you just a moment more
- - for I am looking for myself.

⚜

If you would walk without crutches;
first give away your shoes.

⚜

Simplicity is complex
to those who must learn
instead of know.

And thus it will follow
    if we can just see -
that my mirror of you
     is your mirror of me.

✧

I
am my problem.
I
am my solution.
I
am my goal.
I
am the reason that I don't find me.

✧

In time I will forget what you have said;
  but I will always remember
     whether you believed it or not.

Knowing is a child;
sired by love,
- - but delivered through fear.

❖

How very lucky is the lame man,
for he can see his crutches
and recognise his twisted legs.

❖

Judge me - please;
that I might know the me within you
- - and the you within myself.

❖

How sad can it be
if you can laugh about it later?

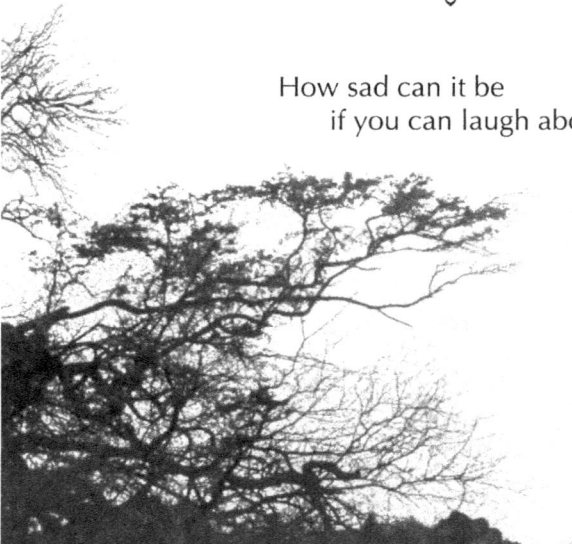

If you would know the worst about you.
    seek those who would war with you;
for your friends are made shy with love
    and their lips are sealed against you.

❖

There will be a time when all things will be known.
Wait upon that time then
        for all love will then be.

❖

The cross has been carried to its full and complete end,
    there is no need to carry it farther.
Is it not now to lift down your own cross and be free then
    that he might not have died in vain?

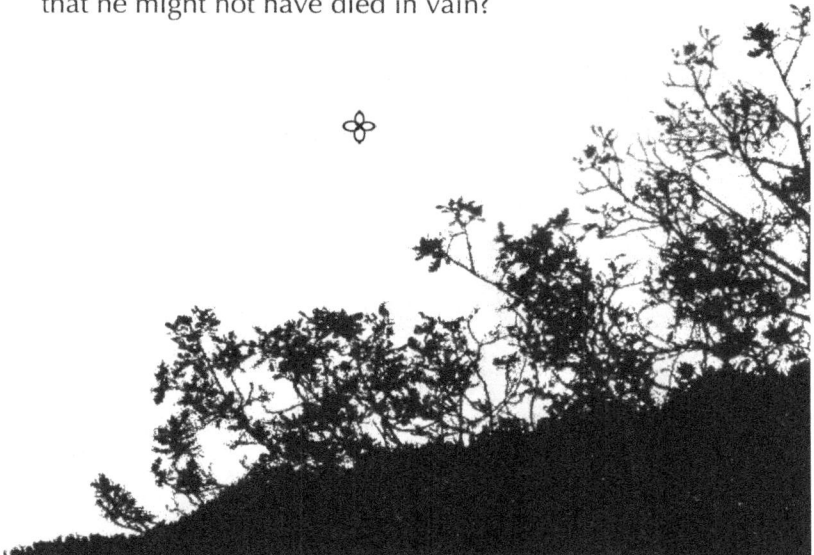

❖

Open your eyes to your ugliness
    and perhaps you will catch a glimpse
      of your beauty.

❀

I said unto the mountain,
    "Move hence."
And the mountain answered saying,
    "Surely master, but won't you lead the way
      that I might follow?

❀

I know enough
to know that I don't know enough,
because I know too much,
  - - yet, not enough.

I love you for my beauty.
    I hate you for my faults.
        I understand in you, that which I have been.
           I fear in you, that which I might become.
Without your reflection of me I would never have known.

❖

    How loudly we yell
        to keep from hearing
           the silence of truth.

❖

    Be yourself.
Don't worry, the blindness that I have to my own beauty
    will protect me from your glory.

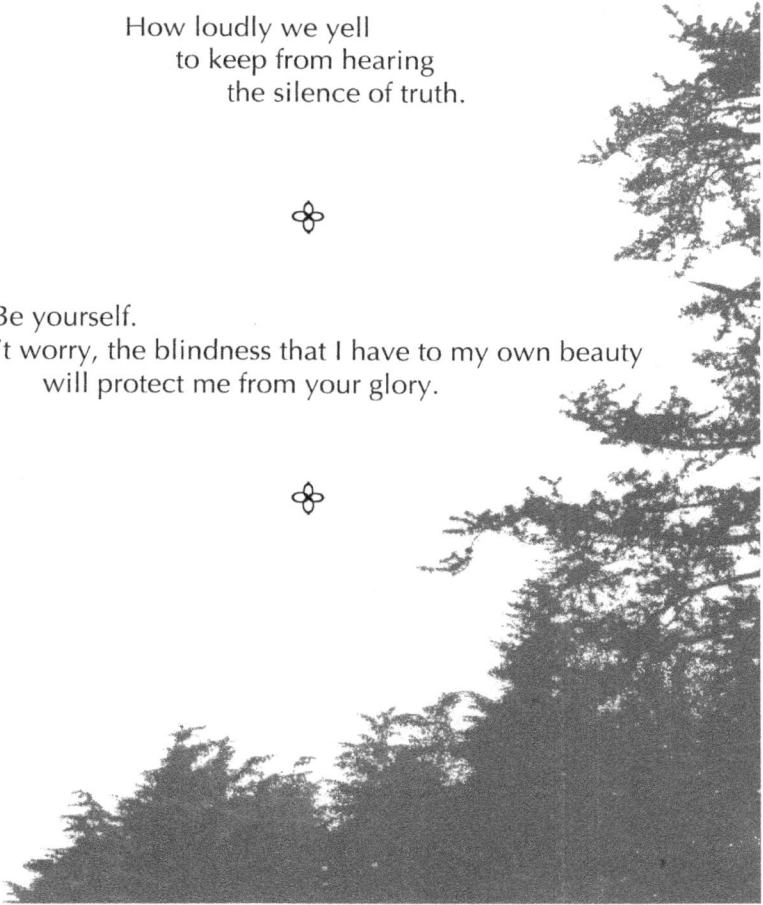

❖

Most of what we say is clever riddles
meant to bedazzle the world.
And that which remains is usually whispered
lest we be listening.

❖

There is a point of crossing over into truth
where the only worry left is that we won't worry
tomorrow about that which worries us today
When that point is reached, gently lift down your cross
from your shoulders and live
while others continue in their own needless
crucifixion.

❖

It is not the giving
nor is it the receiving
but the essence of the gift itself
that is the love.

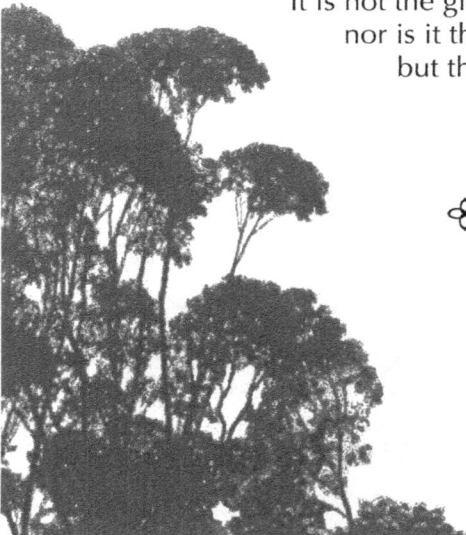

❖

You did not understand,
        perhaps it was too simple.
Let me cloud its beauty with more words
        that you might see it
            - - less beautifully.

✧

            Words are merely spacers
        used to place and thus give meaning
            to the punctuation.

✧

You are always right.
        Is it because you know what you speak
            or that you speak what you know?
And yet you said nothing, what of that?

I have seen but one key to truth;
and that is the word
"I."

❖

There is a newer math,
yet, it is as old as time itself.
In the newer math, one plus one equals one.
Add more ones and the sum remains one,
for we are all One - with.

❖

When at last we speak the truth
it is in our own language that only we feel
and understand.
- - And it is done without words.

❖

The farther you progress
    the less you become,
        yet oh so much more than you were.

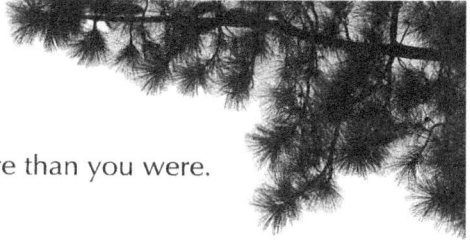

❖

All that we are now, we have always been.
All of that which we are to be, we are now.
    Yet, when we reach "I am,"
we will be so little of that which we have become
    and still we will be all that is.

❖

I know my God and my God knows me
    and we love each other.

❖

I closed my eyes and grew infinite,
endless as God, and on.
And in the nothingness that surrounded me
I saw a spot, so small as only infinites could see.
I knew that spot was me,
- - and it was good.

It truth be silence - -
let us end with the truth of the beginning:
I am my brother, not his brother.
I am my brother.
I am.
I.

✥

Part 2

On the tail of the dragon

Q: Where is God?
A: He is out.
Q: When will He return?
A: When you no longer have to ask.

❖

The waves of the universal sea constantly beat
        upon the shoreline that is mankind.
                The shore resists long and hard, - -
but little by little, grain by grain,
        the shore is carried away by the ever present sea.
                And yet, - -
                        a paradox appears;
        Slowly, each grain finds its own way to the ocean floor,
                to collect there and grow, - - into another shore.

And the waves of the universal sea continue to beat
        upon the shoreline that is mankind.

❖

The beginning of anything new is always now.
    Lives lived in routine can be changed.
        Lives lived buried in debt and problem
          can be turned into freedom.
All it takes is the wanting, and the willingness to forgo
    the chains we have burdened ourselves with.
Look around and see how many are wrapped in their own chains.
    How many are wearing blinders
        to keep from seeing life as it really is?
    Look and see, - -
        then look into a mirror
          and let yourself see again.

    To change your life, just change some habits.

❖

    The bitter taste around the edges at times
        frighten people away
          from some of the best that life has to offer.

❖

We have learned to walk well in the darkness. - -
    Eyes to see
yet the mind's blindfolds conceal what we refuse to perceive.
    Ears to hear
yet the sounds shriek against the brake pads or our mind
    as closed ears refuse to listen.
Other senses guide and direct us around bodies
    of the dead but not forgotten past
        lying just behind the blinders,
            - - the truth lies there as well.

Only when we have accepted our deepest secrets
    can we find true freedom.

It will take great strength and honesty to be free
    and to be that which we truly are.

⬥

Some think that a falsehood can be covered up
by the blinking of an "I."

So many people;
planning plans for tomorrows that never come,
looking for things that they really don't want,
longing for that which they already have,
despising the things they asked for and received,
being people that they are not,
waiting for a savior - while turning strangers from their doors,
   - - and missing the point of it all.

⚜

And yet. - -
What is life but a school?
What is pain but a reminder?
And what are other people but mirrors of ourselves?
   For what, do you suppose? Not for a joke
 but for a lesson to be learned
   or a guidepost along our pathways.

Listen, - - to yourself.
Feel that which you feel, and respond
   that you might grow and rise up
and finally be that which you are.

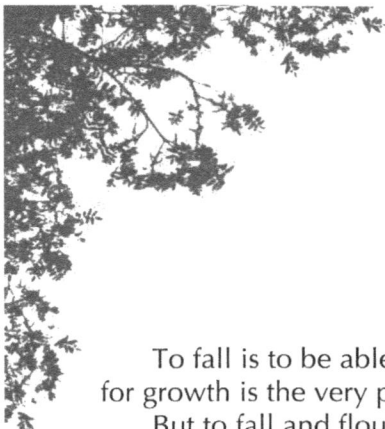

A grudge held is like a fire - -
that burns,
but consumes not.

❖

To fall is to be able to rise again, higher than before,
for growth is the very purpose of the falling.
But to fall and flounder in its depths is to deny the challenge
and take a step backwards
- - and a mighty step it will be.

❖

Some day we may look straight into another's eyes.
But this will not be easy, fot therein truth is found,
and so we practice for a time,
- - by looking away.

❖

Give your eyes a break, - - shed a tear.

You have called it - "victory."
Yet - -
the cost of the victory has been the defeat of another.
Does not the very word then
sound hollow within the depths of your soal?

✤

Oh sure, - -
there is always another time than now, - -
later, - -
when the price won't be quite as dear
- - and the rewards not quite as great.

✤

Feelings kept within are like seeds,
germinating - - or decaying
in the depths of the darkness.

Must we be as warriors when we meet, -
with armor to protect, and stabbing words kept ready
- - just in case?

❖

To give up the battle - -
                is the greatest victory ever won by any warrior.

❖

So very much happens every day.
So many things slip by without being noticed.
Would that we could note the really important things:
     The smile that says, "Can't we be friends?'
     The small pain that says to watch the diet.
     The touch that says, "I know."
But the important things usually slip by,
     too quietly in fact to be noticed by those who are too busy
          with work or with plans
               to see, to feel or to recognise,
                    - - the really important things.

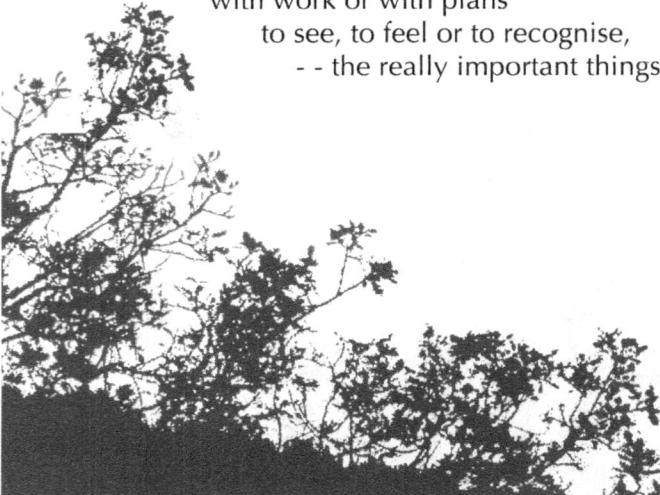

The man walked many times around the great cathedral,
for he wanted and needed a quiet communication with his god.
He had tried each of the huge iron doors but they were all locked.
So the man walked slowly away,
- - for it was closing time.

❖

There will be a way, - -
or perhaps there already is,
and we just don't know where to look.

❖

Tears - -
are the gentle sharing of your soul.

❖

That some give so much with so little
and others give so little with so much,
is mystery,
- - until love is known.

Love is not born
　　but grows from a speck of dust
　　　or a blade of grass
　　　　or anything that "is".

❖

it matters not where you are,
　　what you have or who you might be;
　　without someone to share it,
　You are nowhere, you have nothing,
　　and you are no one at all.

❖

Friends, it seems,
　　are made in minutes.
Acquaintances however,
　　　- - sometimes take years.

❖

There are subtle differences beteween right and wrong,
    what to do and what to avoid.

    If many look at one thing
there will be as many different "sightings"
    as there are eyes to see.

Many are the writings on this subject
    and many are the advocates of each thought.
        - - and yet, there are still judges.

⚜

    Cry when tears form
and seek the way to the source of the flow.

⚜

        Be it one or be it all,
            all is one and one is all.
        Be it single, be it thrice,
            Love is one,
                - - it's kind of nice.

Please don't try to lead me in my life,
for don't you see?
If I followed your directions
it would rob me of my right to live it.

⟡

Being yourself is the greatest work of art that can be.
Being yourself inspires more feeling than a great
    opera or artist's masterwork.
Being yourself is the greatest challenge and most difficult
    task ever set for mankind.
Being yourself - -
    - - is the real reason for being.

⟡

We are only as close as we allow each other
- - to "be".

⟡

Love is truth and truth is love,
and that which is less
- - is less.

❖

If God is all things - -
(and could "He" be less?)
"He" would have to be all evil as well as all good.
Who then, should fear judgement day more than "He"?
Resolve then to forgive your god,
and perhaps "He" will do likewise.

❖

God is love.
God is truth.
Love is truth.
God is all things
and all things are love.
All things are truth,
What then of a lie?

Is there no one who understands?
Perhaps it is that no one *can* understand.
Perhaps is it that when we say to another, "understand me",
　　we are asking them to do something that we ourselves
　　　　- - have not accomplished.

⚜

It has been the pattern of parents, churches and teachers
　　to cause children to control their words and actions.
"Do this", "Don't do that" and "We don't talk about that"
　　have taught most of us to become *controled*.
This makes for a more socially acceptable person,
　　but what of the feelings we keep within?
　　　　What of the words we do not speak?
We were born doing and saying what we felt,
　　until we again regain that which we were born with
　　we shall never be free.

⚜

Feel, don't think, and do what you feel.
And follow your feelings if your feelings are real.

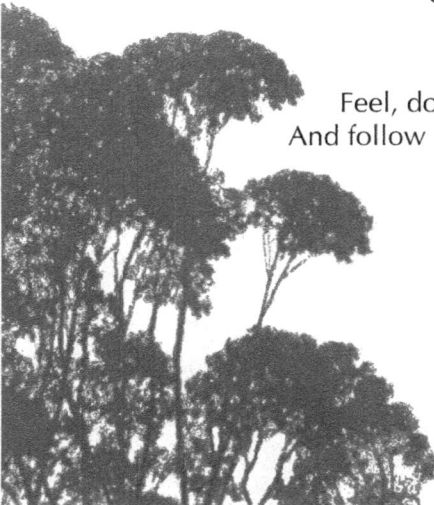

Follow what your feelings say:
Feel work, work. Feel play, play.
Feel glad, laugh. Feel bad, cry.
Feel life, live. Feel dead, die.
      Feel lonely - - ?

❖

      Follow me - -
I am your tears.
      Follow me - -
I am your happiness and your joy.
      Follow me - -
I am your feelings.
I am your signposts to yourself.
      Follow me - -
I will lead you to God.

❖

   Many times have made but once.
  And only once,
has also made many times.

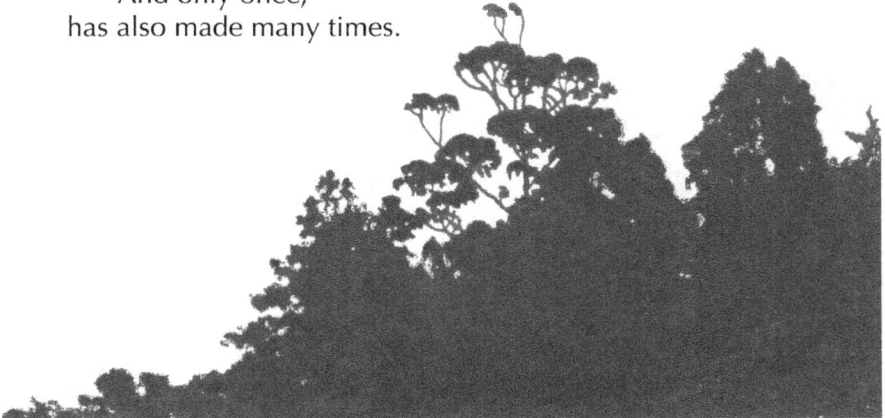

We are the leaders of ourselves, - -
     and the followers too,
          and the stragglers behind.
Keen then in step with yourself
     and follow not the dreams of the masses
          nor the maps of the wise;
for you alone can chart, follow and walk
          - - upon your own pathway.

⚜

My heart was made hard,
     and I cried unto God,
          "Give, give, why must I always give,
               when lord, will be my turn to receive?"
Then a silence came over me,
     and a small voice whispered gently from within;
          "That which you have given
               did you not first receive?"
     - - And my silence was filled.

⚜

I feared that I might die, - - soon,
     and it gave me courage
          to face more of life.

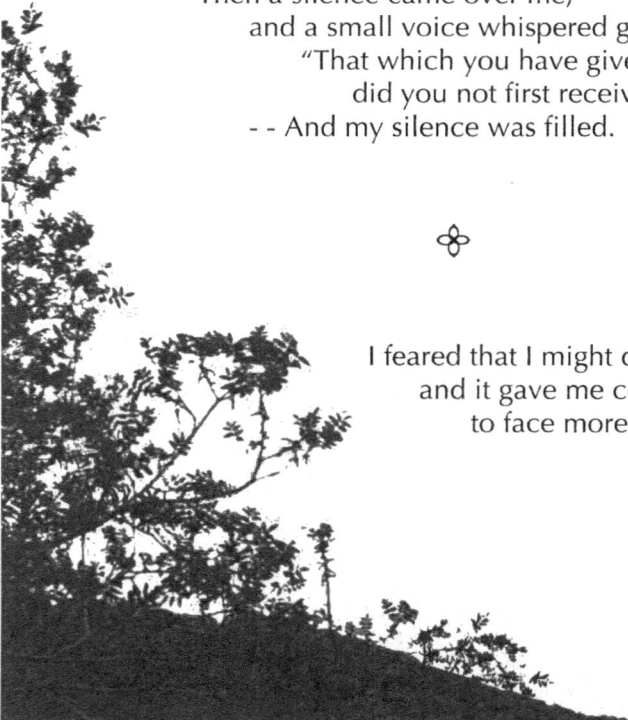

At both extremes of emotion there are tears;
tears of happiness and tears of sorrow and despair.
This is a good thing then,
for tears wash the soul.

❖

Burn not your bridges,
yet - seek not to cross them again.
- - ahead is the way.
What is done is done and ever shall be.
The way ahead is filled with all things - -
the way behind is past.
To return is to bind the chains ever tighter.
Ask what is gained by returning,
and if the answer is hollow,
walk onward into the sunlight of a new day.

❖

He who does not face life
- - does not live life.

It is not in the plan of things
that we always know the plan of things.

❧

We are all limited by that which we are, and what we represent;
wear a smile on your face and find people smiling back,
wear a frown and meet disgruntled and unhappy people.
If we live a lie we will not know who or what we are.
If we are honest we know truth.
If we are free we know freedom.
The world that surrounds us is very much a mirror of ourselves.
It has been said "It takes a thief to know a thief".
- - It is likewise with saints.

❧

If you do not wish to be compared to someone
do not try to take their place.

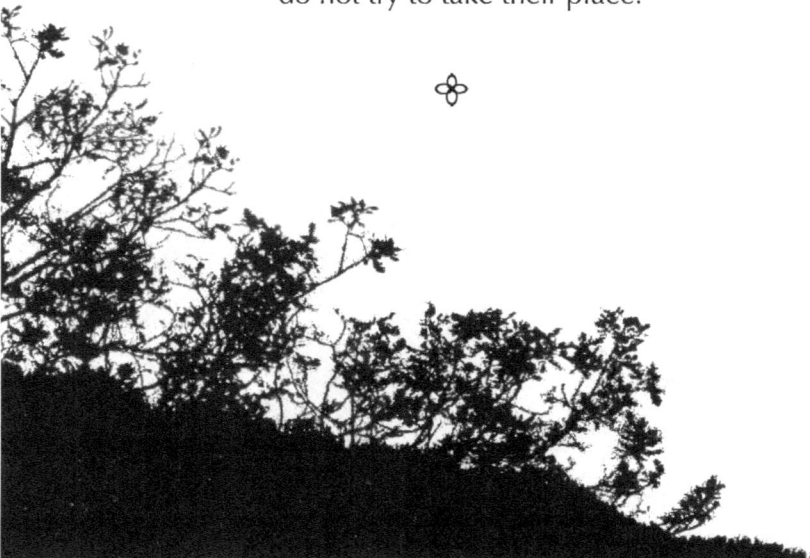

❧

❀

As you love. so you love.
As you love, have you love.
As you love, with you love.
As you love, for you love.
As you love, you love.
As you love,
you love
you.

❀

Just know and be responsible for what it is that you do
and you will be able to calm the waves of karma.

❀

Living is not planning, nor waiting for the dawn.
Living if not fearing things to be.
Nor us it reminiscing of days so long, long gone,
but doing what we can do now
with what we have
- - you see?

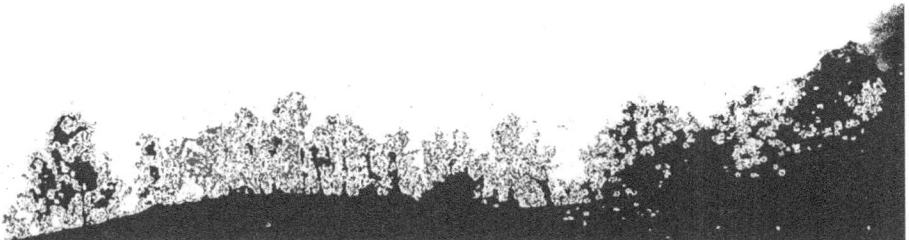

Why does God come so unexpectedly?
Just when we give up and begin to do it ourselves
"He" lends a hand.

⚜

Things we don't talk about
        lie hiding behind blinders of our minds,
            and shame hides there as well.
There are many walls in our minds;
        built over the years as protection
            for our seemingly fragile selves.
        The truth of who we are
            also lies hidden among them.

When the blinders have been removed from our eyes
        and the walls have been torn down
            we can learn to walk in freedom;
        leaving many of the old laws and ways of living behind..,
not because they were false,
        but because we have outgrown them.
And once our tongues have learned to speak the truth
        do we finally hear and learn the truth
            - - which we have spoken to ourselves.

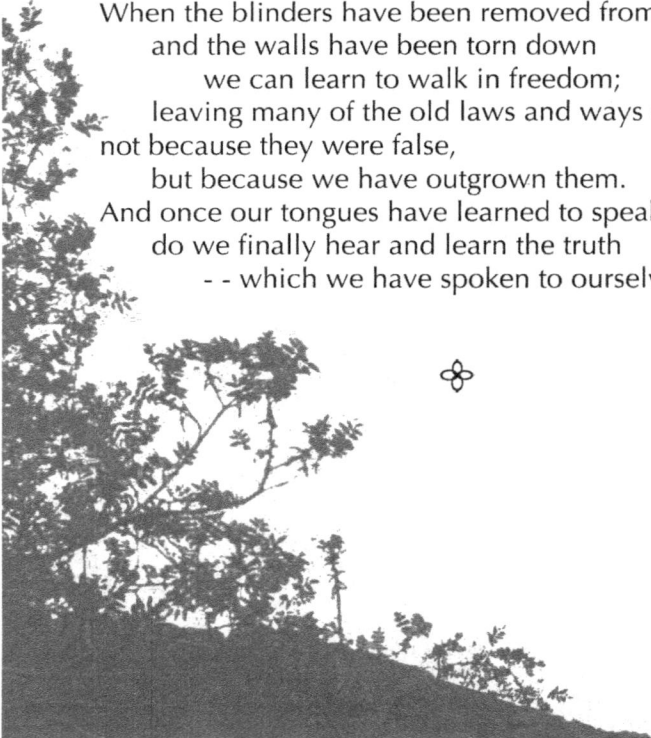

⚜

Close not your eyes to the world,
    - - yet,
close your eyes to seek the world within,
      therein lies the truth.
The world that we see cannot be trusted
      for we see and hear what we want and expect.
We are also guided by those who want us to see and hear
      the things of their own experience.

Without external eyes to confound us
      we are able to finally see
           and all things can be known.

It is not easy to do these things;
      to know, to be free
           nor is it easy to truly love.

It takes strength, resolution
      and an honest look at yourself to do these things;
         - - to let go of what is
            in exchange for what can be..

❖

Judgement day has come, - - it is here now.
You have built your own temple
    with your words and your deeds
      and judgement is nothing more
        than to dwell within its walls.

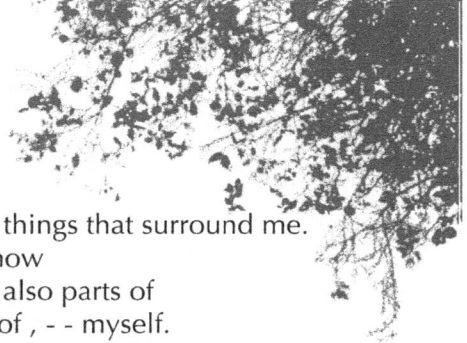

I know that I am only a part of the things that surround me.
And yet, - - somehow I also know
that these same things are also parts of
- - and even wholes of , - - myself.

❖

Many are the ways of God.
Many are the masks and faces.
Many can be one in all things.
You can make many into One,
by being One with,
instead of being one apart.

❖

What if Christ was just a guy like me?

❖

We are a product of all that we have been.
We are all that we have been.
We are all that we have.
We are all.
We are.
- - All.

❖

Part 3

- - And life goes on

Indeed it is better to discover that which is
than to wait upon that which is not.

❀

I don't get it
- - a lot.

Here, catch ! - -

- - Got it.

❀

Do you see the dawn
- - right here in my eyes.
I have seen the end of a night.
I was the one who put the darkness out
by waking up

I just saw another dawn
upon the image of living
through the eyes of being.

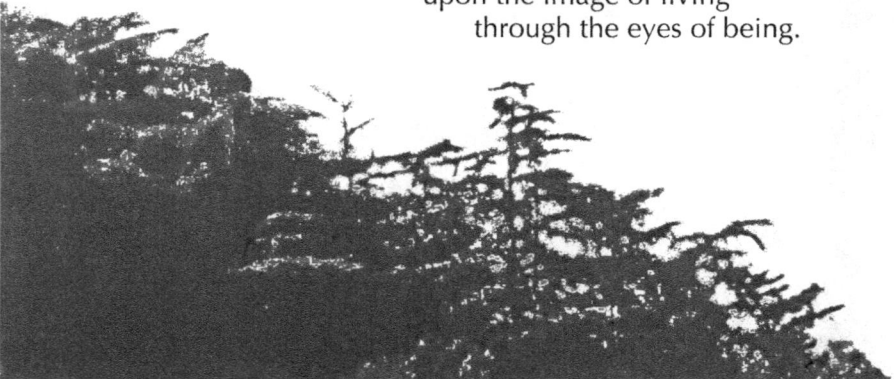

Come one come all, and open hand awaits.
Come friends and lovers, hear my call
- - and let us share our separate fates.

✿

There is something that sings
within and empty spot in me.

✿

I feel as a lonely dog howling at the moon:
flying on dreams of imagination.
I spend sleepness nights with empty fullness.

✿

How can I stay still
as cupid draws his string
- - again.

I am as old as time and as young as this moment.
I am ageless, ever changing, ever changeless.

❖

Time in its jagged flight
lightnings throgh the cosmos of my mind
light memories of a storm
- - just passed.

❖

I feel the blocks, placed by my own hasty hand.
I have erred much, - - and yet I persevered;
- - and I have cursed the error in the name of perseverance.

❖

Feelings are not to be judged
for they are the signposts of life.

Would the shaft be pointed true
and pointed in its weathered flight;
into the very core, heart and soul
- - of he who loosed the bow.

❖

To think a bad thought is the easiest thing;
to think good thoughts however,
sometimes requires more effort.

❖

Slivers are funny things;
sometimes we don't even notice them entering the skin.
Why is it they hurt most as they are being pulled out?
Some people are like slivers.

❖

A society that does not recognise
hard work and excellence
creates its own decay.

The world is not limited by your vision of it,
yet your world view is limited by your vision of it.
Both are true,
- - yet each vision is ever changing.

⚜

All of my "now-ness" gives expression
to alll of my pasts.

⚜

Be here, in this place, in the now.
This moment will never be again,
- - yet, it will never end.

⚜

Change - oh change, you thief of pasts and guardian of futures;
- - how subtly your knife severs the cords of the complacent
Change, - oh change
How is it that you alone
stand unchanging?

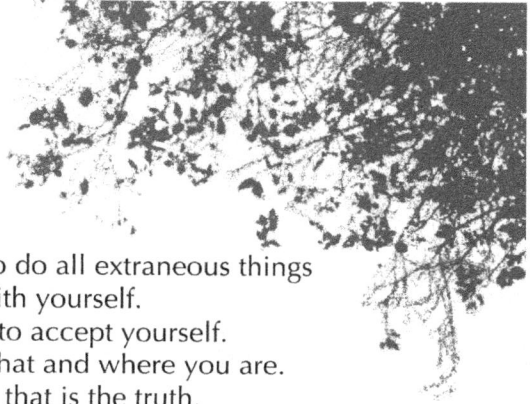

The job is not bo try to do all extraneous things
but to be One whith yourself.
To know and to accept yourself.
as who,what and where you are.
- - for that is the truth.

✤

No one said the hard times would be easy.
- - yet, there is no better time than now.

There is no arduous work, only ardusous attitude;
and no one is a failure who tries.

✤

If you can sleep at night
with no need to wake with mornings light.
Yet greet the morning sun with joy and expertatins tor the new day
have you not then discovered one of the great joys
of living?

✤

A smile costs you nothing,
a frown however, can be much more expensive.

It is not what we have that makes us rich
it is what we give away.

✧

Many churches talk about a veil which is lifted at death.
I have seen through that which is called the veil.
It was simply a process
of looking beyond the three dimensions.

✧

Who says you have to lay down your body to die?
You could actually change your life - -
or what we hippies used to call, *stepping out*.
Leaving a life that you have created and entering a new one
can involve changing your friends;
actually moving to another place,
or just leaving.
Once in the new life,
the only thing holding you to your old life
is your habits.

✧

Some people stay with us no matter what we do
or where we go, in life and afterwords;
these people are our soul-mates.

❖

Death depends upon the focus that is placed upon it.
There are many deaths,
     one of them includes the laying down of the body.
There are many deaths where change, could be counted
               as death.
     We die many deaths each day.
Life is a series of dying and being reborn.
Cells are being renewed in our bodies every second.
Over a period of years most of the body has simply been replaced.
     - - and the atoms continue to "work" even when we are dead.
               Where then is the death?

❖

Which part of you at this moment is not dying
and being reborn or replaced?
Are you less the molecules that are dying this minute
     than your heart, your nose or your eye?
               Who are you?
          Should you cut yourself and a drop of blood falls,
     is that drop of blood not you as well?

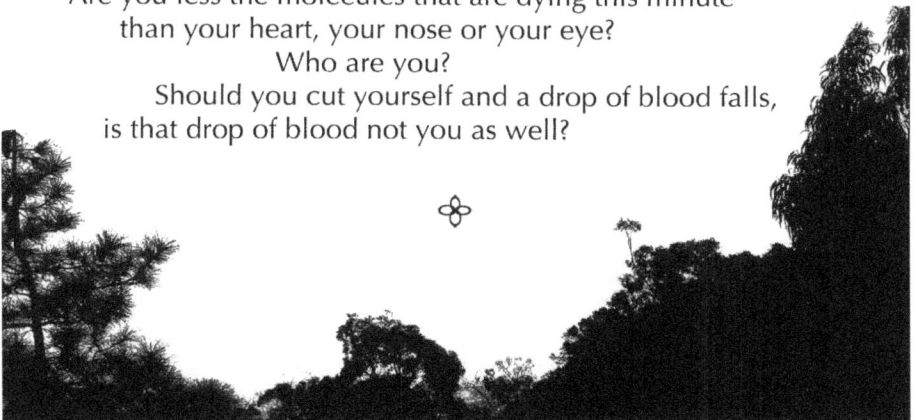

❖

What we see going on today has been going on
in many ways, many places and with many different characters
since the beginning of mankind.
As long as there is a thought of "being better than,"
there will always be this strife,
be it between a few people or world wide.

⊰⊱

Fear - is the energy to do our best in new situations.
Guilt - is the energy for personal growth.
Unworthiness - keeps us on track.
Hurt feelings - remind us how much we care.
Anger - is the energy for change.
Discouragement - reveals our courage.
Failure - is a firm foundation to grow anew.

⊰⊱

Nothing is free;
first you must climb the mountain
before you can stand on its top.

Time is an illusion which allows us to generate
    a linear vision of reality.
We need this because our minds are set
    upon a three dimentional reality.
Time will also make all things true,
    the thought itself has created the possibility.

✤

God doesn't do things *for* you, God does things *with* you.

✤

What is your relationship with God?
    And what is God all about for you?
The way you think about God determines how you experience God.

✤

You don't have to have a religion to know God,
you just have to be honest with yourself.
Open your eyes and take an honest look at yourself
and you can know all things.

⚜

I tell you, you cannot know more of God
than you know of your self.

⚜

No man achieves good by worshiping another man or God,
for in doing so he makes himself separate - - and less.

⚜

The word "God" is very limiting.
It is so because each time the word is used
people tend to picture a different and limited thing.
What if God is endless?
What if the cosmos and all of its contents are God?
What if God is All That Is?

We are all a part of All that Is,
therefore we can never be apart from All That Is.

⊕

In the entire universe there is not another you.
hence you are perfect as you are.
Each of us adds our own personal element to All That Is.
How could it be complete without a *you*?

⊕

The word Christ is a title, not a person.
There have been and still are, many Christs.

⊕

All about you you see mirrors of yourself,
it is this way with everyman.

⊕

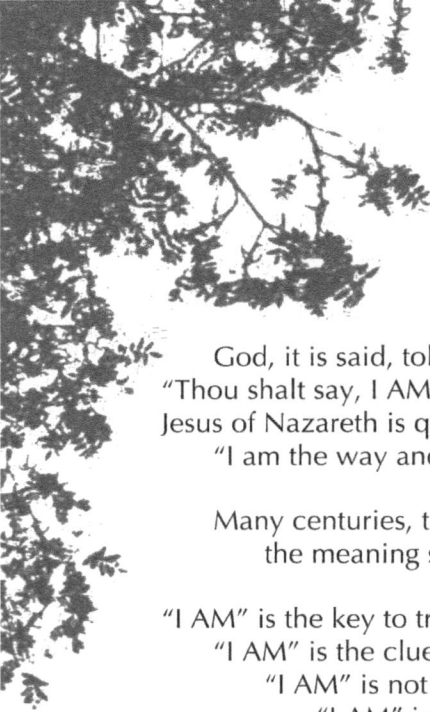

God, it is said, told Moses,
"Thou shalt say, I AM, I AM hath come to you."
Jesus of Nazareth is quoted as saying,
    "I am the way and the light."

Many centuries, translations and re-writings later
    the meaning seems to have been lost.

"I AM" is the key to truth and knowing.
    "I AM" is the clue.
        "I AM" is not someone else.
            "I AM" is You
        said from and to yourself.

You are "I AM".

❖

Afterword

First I want to apologise for the use of
"he, him, his and man;"
- - a limitation of the English language.

❖

I believe that we are each
in charge of our own progression.
That we can choose to better ourselves as we see fit
or leave it to our spiritual selves to sort it out
as the veil is lifted away
and all is revealed.

MF/BB

❖

www.ingramcontent.com/pod-product-compliance
Lightning Source LLC
Chambersburg PA
CBHW020516030426
42337CB00011B/423